A Poetics of Space

Pavement Books
London, UK
www.pavementbooks.com

British Library Cataloguing in Publication Data.
A catalogue record for this book is available from the British Library.

ISBN: 978-0-9571470-2-7

A Poetics of Space

Images of Côn Đảo

Contents

Preface 1

Towards a poetics of space 5
Sophie Fuggle

In search of a Name... 13
Sophie Fuggle

From darkness to light: Portrait pictures in the Bảo Tàng Côn Đảo Museum 23
Maryse Tennant

Nature reserve 31
Katharina Massing

The carceral archipelago of the dead: On the singularity of Hàng Dương cemetery 37
Charles Forsdick

Acknowledgments 48

Preface

Before we visited Côn Đảo in September 2018, we held a number of preconceived ideas about what we imagined we would see and experience. The infamous *Life Magazine* images of the Tiger Cages played a key role in framing our imagination of the island's horrific past. Those of us who have visited other former French penal colonies anticipated a similar example of a prison island rehabilitated as a tropical paradise to those we have seen in New Caledonia and French Guiana. Yet what we saw challenged many of our preconceptions.

We have all talked at length about the island but are all struggling in different ways to know how and what to articulate. This exhibition and accompanying catalogue are a first attempt to do so.

Prior to arriving in Hồ Chí Minh City, Charles Fox was working in Phnom Penh, Cambodia, a space that he has been working in as a photographer for the last 13 years, questioning the legacies of conflict and colonialism. As a result of a brief encounter with a foreign correspondent based in Phnom Penh who had written a piece on Côn Đảo for an English language paper, he learned there were still a handful of former prisoners living on the island. This insight radically changed our collective thinking about Côn Đảo. As it turned out there were five former prisoners in all, four men and a woman. They are occasionally mentioned in the glossy, Sunday supplement features that refer to Côn Đảo as the Devil's Island of Vietnam. But the presence of these people when referenced is evoked only as folklore. No international journalists it seemed, at least in recent years, had ever met with the former prisoners. The pristine beaches and Six Senses resort where Brad and Angelina once vacationed were clearly more worthy of column inches, a more appealing consumable narrative.

Discussions shifted back and forth from the representation of incarceration to what it might mean to meet, talk with and photograph the former prisoners? With a mixture of excitement and trepidation we debated the realities and ethical questions around seeking out these individuals and asking them to be photographed... Perhaps there was a good reason why no foreign journalists had been to see them before?

On a dismal rainy afternoon that bore no resemblance to the idyllic beach scenes presented in Lonely Planet, we took a guided tour of the main sites on the island belonging to the former French prison. The light was poorer than usual inside the cells and the English speaking guide was impatient to get us around the site while we discussed amongst ourselves what to make, if anything, of the shackled, emaciated mannequins intended to bring the scene to life. However, at some point something happened. Suddenly, thanks to Đặng Thị Kim Phụng, our colleague at Tôn Đức Thắng University, our guide was on his mobile to the daughter of one of the former prisoners. Before we knew it Charles and Kim Phụng had a meeting arranged to see him the next morning. By the time next morning arrived, the other four had learned of Charles' project and were also keen to meet and talk to him and Kim Phụng.

Their collective narrative dissects perceptions of the island. How did Côn Đảo become home for the five former prisoners who were asked to stay and build a community in a space that once imprisoned and tortured them? This question challenges commonplace perceptions about the site which is not one simply of memory or, for those that visit the beach resorts, forgetting. The presence of the former prisoners on the island profoundly changed how we saw the space and has led us to ask new questions. What does it mean to stay rather than leave a site of suffering like Côn Đảo? What kind of individual and collective strength can be found in turning a space once associated with exile and abandonment into one of family and belonging?

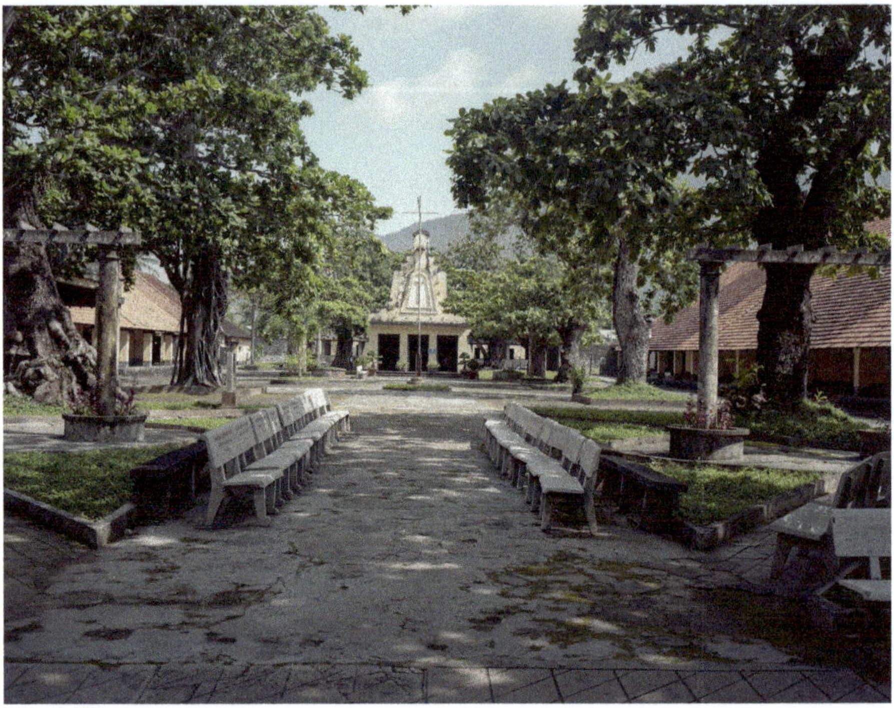

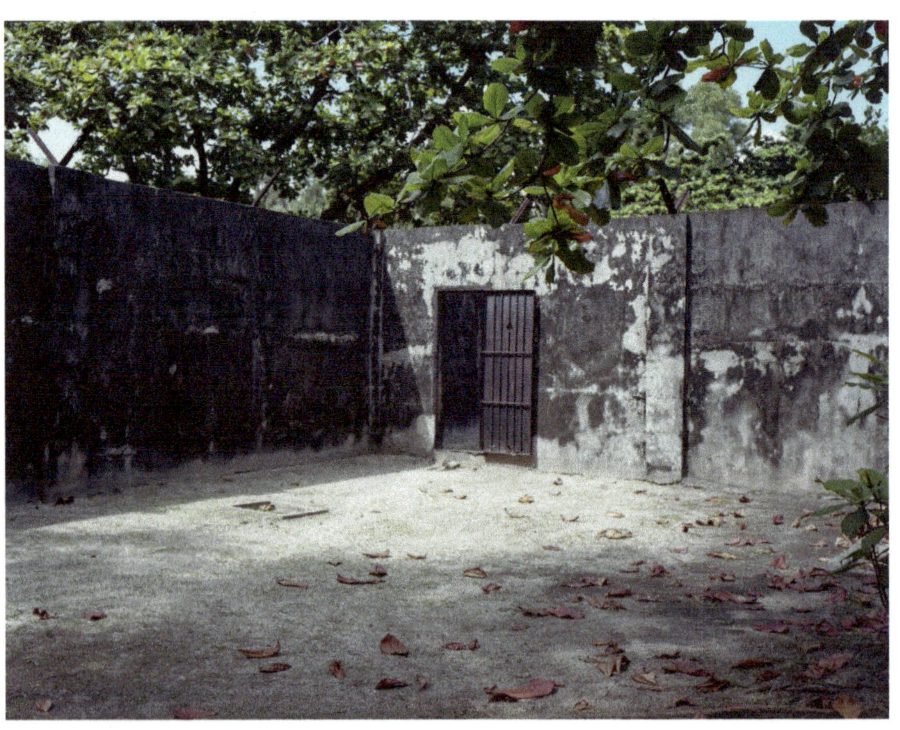

Towards a poetics of space

Towards a poetics of space

It is not mere coincidence or shameless appropriation that the title of the exhibition, A Poetics of Space, makes allusion to Gaston Bachelard's 1958 text, *The Poetics of Space*. Published at the very moment when France was in the process of withdrawing its colonial occupation from Vietnam as well as elsewhere, Bachelard's celebration of the poetic imagination of space offers a nostalgic reading of modes of living associated particularly with a French rural landscape. At first glance, to evoke such a reading that evacuates what he refers to as 'hostile spaces' from its narrative seems counterintuitive within the context of Côn Đảo and its difficult, violent histories. Moreover, Bachelard seems perhaps to offer a romantic affirmation of all that had been lost by the French during and after the Second World War. What relevance, if any, is there in applying Bachelard's *topophilia* to the space of Côn Đảo?

It is in its emphasis on the lived experience of space and specifically the idea of 'dwelling' that Bachelard's text most resonates with our project. It calls to account any analysis we carry out purely from the outside and challenges us to think beyond a straightforward geometry of space. The former prisoners who remained on Côn Đảo bear witness to a dwelling that is far more complex than the reveries of the childhood homestead described by Bachelard. It is as a lived or embodied experience, whether this be short or long-term, that we hope to better get to grips with what Côn Đảo has, does and might mean.

As Peter Zinoman has argued in *The Colonial Bastille*, French colonial prisons in Vietnam were not simply sites of extreme suffering due to overcrowding, limited rations and the unpredictable violence meted out by the guards and *caplans*. They were also sites where many prisoners experienced their political education and developed forms of anti-colonial resistance. As such, Côn Sơn (or Poulo-Condore) prison was an intense space of writing. Several clandestine newspapers circulated. Extracts from key political writings were marked onto cell walls. On release from Côn Sơn in 1921 where he had spent thirteen years, Huỳnh Thúc Kháng founded the newspaper *Tiếng Dân* (The Voice of the People). Between 1937 and 1938, the paper published a series of poems written by those who had spent time in the prison. Notable amongst these is Phan Châu Trinh's *đập đá Côn Lôn* which has been translated by Huỳnh Sanh Thông as *Breaking Rocks on Con Dao*:

> A man stands tall upon Con Dao
> he makes a din that makes a mountain shake.
> Hammer to shatter heap on heap of rocks.
> Break stone by hand to hundreds of small chips.
> To granite turn your body day by day.
> Can sun or rainstorm daunt an iron heart?
> When they're laid low, those who will save the world
> will endure and let no trifle bother them.

Interestingly, the image presented here is not one of cells and confinement but rather the island itself conceived as prison. Its topography and climate define the physical suffering of the prisoners but one that is met with solid rock-like resistance. The hostility of the island is presented as test, a form of training for those 'who will save the world.' The man seems to absorb the properties of the island without conforming to the limits of its space.

It is perhaps only in terms of a poetics that the hostility of the island as prison can simultaneously be read as a site of self-transformation and resistance. A poetics refuses a single, fixed meaning and thus refuses an affirmation or acceptance of the French and American prison buildings that continue to scar the landscape. A poetics can describe a space whilst refusing its description. As the character Esternome tells his daughter in Patrick Chamoiseau's *Texaco* in relation to a different form of French colonial imprisonment, the slace dungeon or *cachot*:

> Allow me not to go into details about the dungeon, Marie-Sophie, because you see those things are not to be described. Lest we ease the burden of those who built them.

Sophie Fuggle

References

Bachelard, Gaston, *The Poetics of Space* (Boston, MA: Beacon Press, 1994 [1958]).

Chamoiseau, Patrick, *Texaco*, translated from the French by Rose-Myriam Réjouis and Val Vinokurov (London: Granta, 1997 [1992]).

Kháng, Huỳnh Thúc, *Thi tù tùng thoại* [Prison Verse] (Hue: NXB Tieng Dan, 1939).

Thông, Huỳnh Sanh (editor and translator), *An Anthology of Vietnamese Poems: From the Eleventh Through the Twentieth Centuries* (New Haven, CT: Yale University Press, 1996).

Zinoman, Peter, 'Reading Revolutionary Prison Memoirs,' in *The Country of Memory: Remaking the Past in Late Socialist Vietnam*, edited by Hue-Tam Ho Tai (Berkeley, CA: University of California Press, 2001).

Zinoman, Peter, *The Colonial Bastille: A History of Imprisonment in Vietnam, 1862-1940* (Berkeley, CA: University of California Press, 2001).

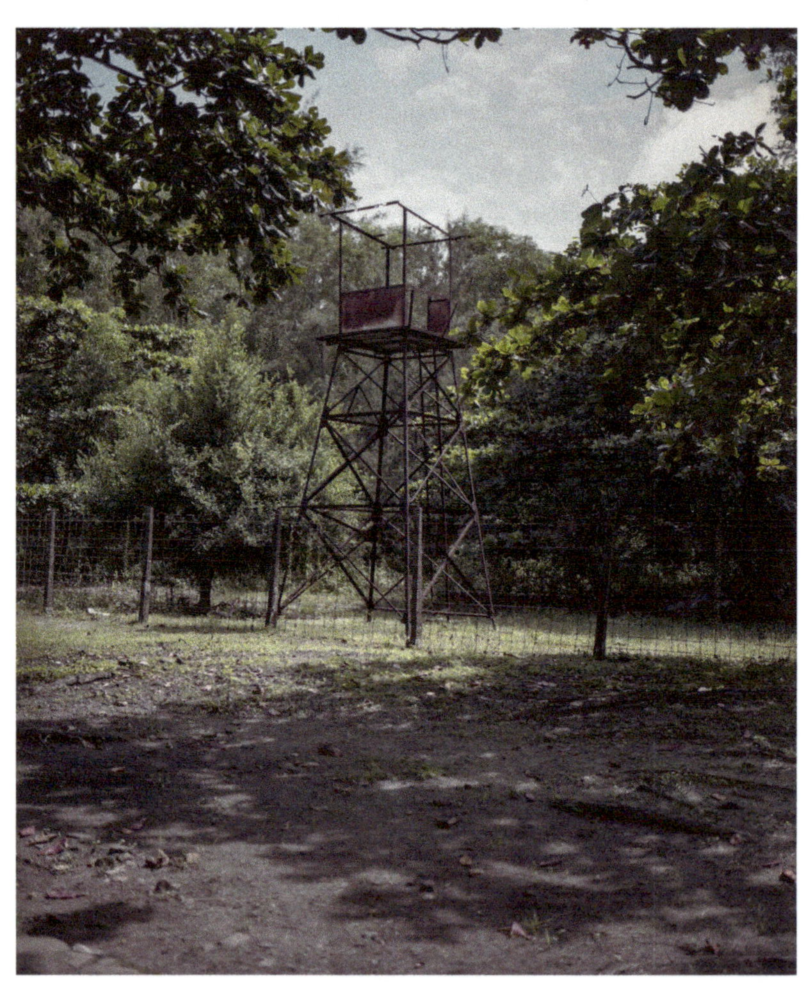

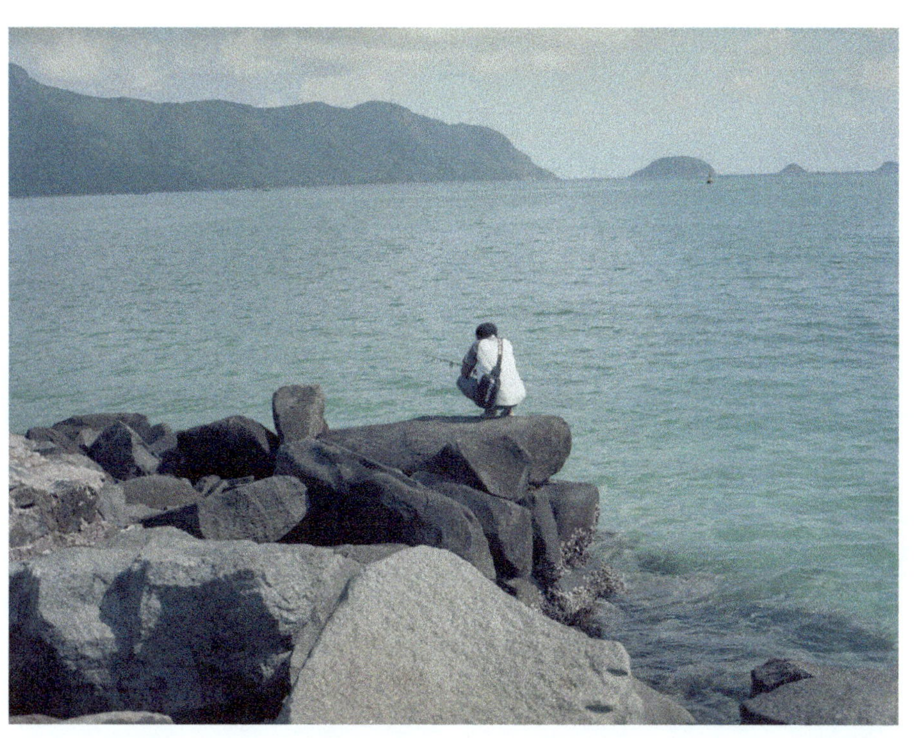

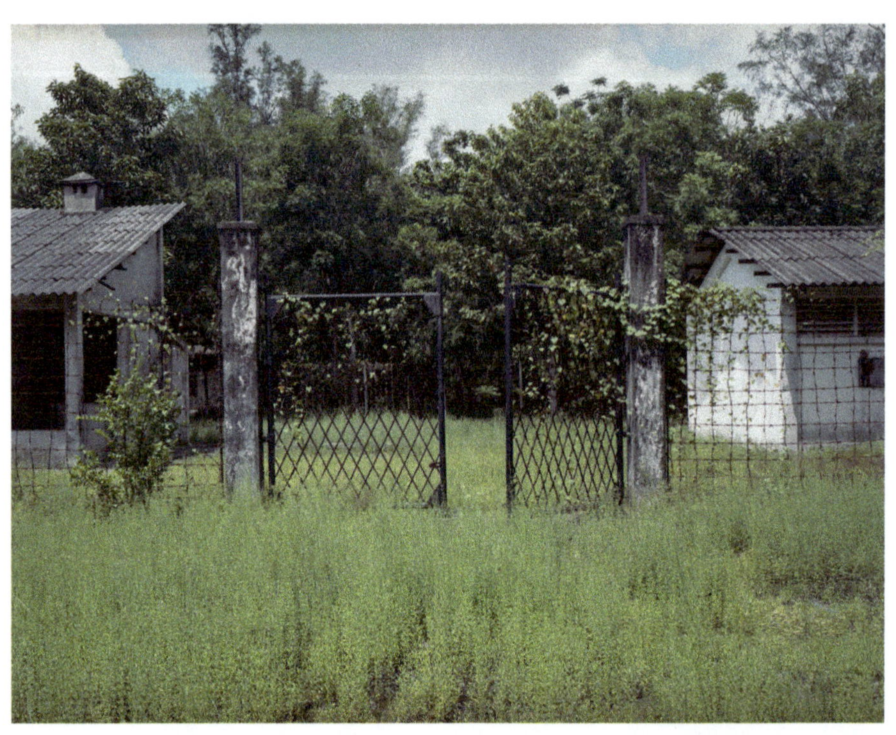

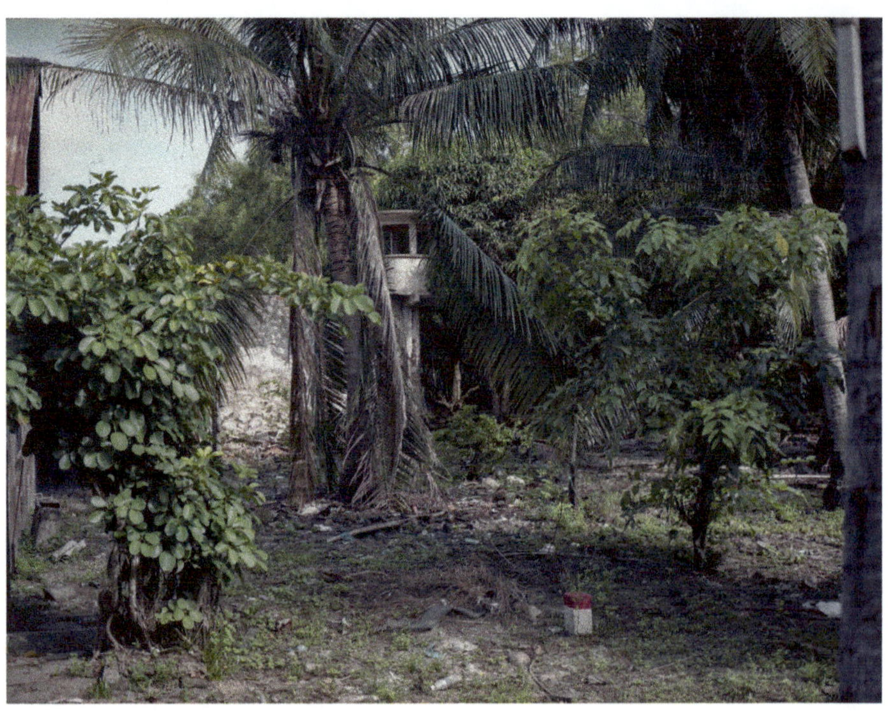

In search of a Name...

In search of a Name...

The geopolitical value of Côn Đảo as a strategic point for explorers throughout history can be traced via clear references to the archipelago from Marco Polo in the 13th Century onwards. Most interesting perhaps is the mythical status apparently attributed to the islands in Ptolemy's Geography where they are possibly the three islands depicted as the Isles of the Satyrs. Adam Anderson's 1764 *Origin of Commerce* specifically evokes the islands in its mockery of the erroneous and fanciful mapmaking efforts of Ptolemy:

> And, to demonstrate how little they knew either eastward or north-eastward of the Aurea Chersonesus, i.e. probably the promontory of Malacca, Ptolemy has placed thereabouts the three fabulous *Isles of the Satyrs*, wherein they supposed the inhabitants to have tails like beasts; and that ships having any iron nails fastened in them were stopped in the neighbouring seas of those isles, and could not proceed, on account of the rocks of loadstone or magnet at the bottom of the sea...

There is little historical consensus on the number of islands making up the archipelago which range from the three referenced by Ptolemy all the way up to the current official total of sixteen. Where all the islands have multiple names, many are little more than large rocks of less than 100 m^2.

Pulo-Condor was the name given to the islands by the British East India Company who set up a short-lived and fateful garrison on Côn Sơn Island in 1702. Pulo is a variation of the Malay 'pulau' meaning 'island'. 'Condore' with its multiple spellings is said to refer to Con Son's gourd-like shape.

However, it is also possible that the island's name evolved from the mythical Chinese place known as 'Kunlun'. 'Kunlun Shan' also refers to 'mountain range' in Mandarin and it is likely that Côn Đảo's mountainous terrain inspired the name 'Kunlun Shan Islands' marked on the 17th Century Mao Kun navigation map compiled by Mao Yuanyi in 1628 and now held in the Library of Congress. In his short book published during his time on the island as prison director, J. Brulé suggests a variation on the transliteration of the Chinese 'K'Ouen Louen', subsequently transformed into Con Non by the Annamites meaning 'island of snakes'.

Variations on Condore [kondor, condur, sondur] have existed since Polo's visit in 1292. However, the name has become inextricably linked to the period in the archipelago's history marked by French colonial rule. The French version, 'Poulo-Condore' functioned and continues to do so in the French imaginary as metonym for the prison established in 1861. The French would also refer to the islands as 'Les Condores' and sometimes Côn Sơn becomes 'Grande Condore' in that context. (Hòn Bà the largest of the small islands and located immediately South West of Côn Sơn was known as Petite Condore.) A travel memoir written in 1723 offers up the suggested nickname of 'Isle d'Orléans en Chine' but this doesn't seem to have taken hold at any point.

Despite its deplorable conditions, the prison was dismissively nicknamed the 'bagne à la noix de coco' [coconut prison] by the French penal administration. The term 'bagne' was adopted from the original 'bagne portuaires', the eighteenth century dockyard prisons located along France's coastline in Rochefort, Brest and Toulon. It was subsequently applied to France's main penal colonies in French Guiana and New Caledonia. A significant number of Vietnamese political prisoners from Poulo-Condore were sent on to French Guiana and New Caledonia. Various administrative tactics were employed to alter their status from 'political prisoner' to 'criminal' thus allowing them to be placed on work detail in the forest camps in French Guiana.

It is not clear when exactly the shift from the French Poulo-Condore to the Vietnamese Con Son took place but it is likely to have been in the mid to late 1950s when France were in the process of withdrawing from Indochine and had given up on the idea of maintaining the islands as a carceral archipelago in Southeast Asia. In CIA bulletins dating from the mid-1960s, the archipelago is marked on the map of Vietnam as 'Con Son' followed by 'Poulo-Condore' in brackets. By the mid-1970s, it is unequivocally referred to as Con Son in US documentation.

Today, to refer to Con Son even when talking specifically about the largest island seems to evoke the horrors of the American War just as Poulo-Condore evokes the atrocities of French colonial occupation. Instead in both tourist literature and general conversation in Vietnam, Con Dao is used as the preferred term.

Sophie Fuggle

References

Archives Nationales d'Outre-Mer, ANOM C11 folios 7-17.

Anderson, Adam, *An Historical and Chronological Deduction of the Origin of Commerce, from the earliest accounts to the present time* (London: A. Millar, 1764).

Brulé, J., *Poulo Condore* (Saigon: Presses Indochinoises, 1947).

Demarivaux, Jean-Claude., *Les Secrets des Îles Poulo-Condore: Le grand bagne Indochinois* (Paris: J. Peyronnet, 1956).

Huan, Ma, *Ying-Yai, sheng-lan: The Overall Survey of the Ocean's Shores*, translated by Feng Ch'eng-Chün with an introduction by J.V.G. Mills (Cambridge: Cambridge University Press, 1970).

Wong Tze-ken, D., 'The Destruction of the English East India Company Factory on Condore Island, 1702-1705', *Modern Asian Studies*. 46:5 (September 2012): 1097-1115.

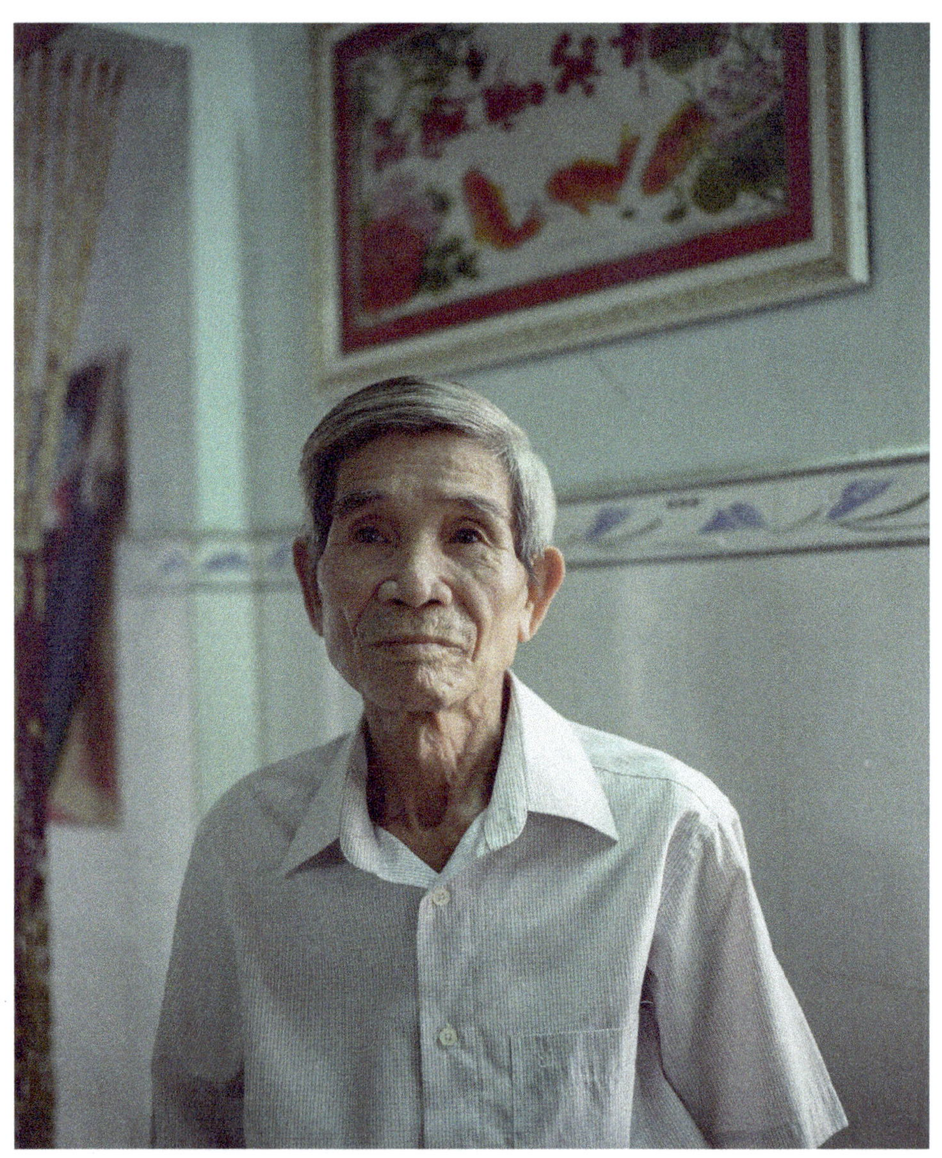

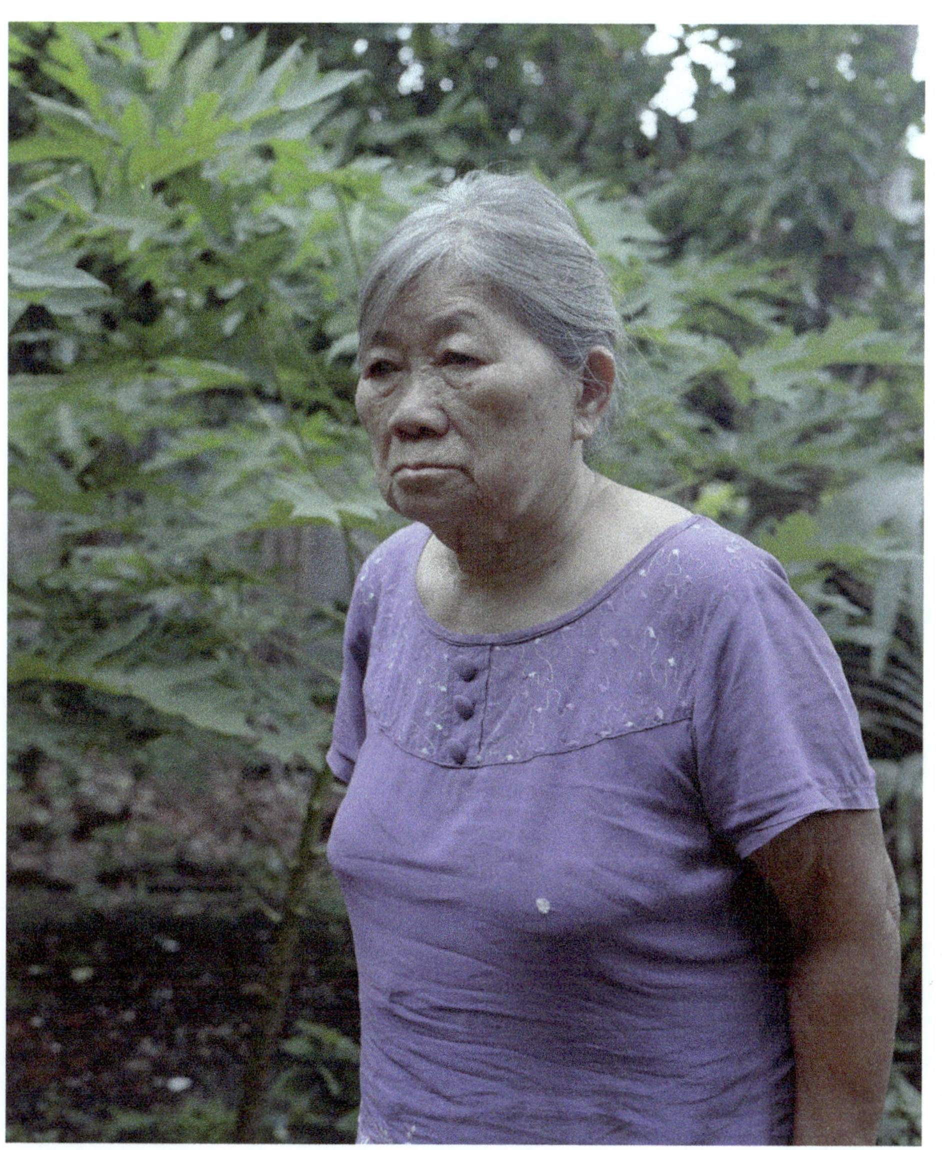

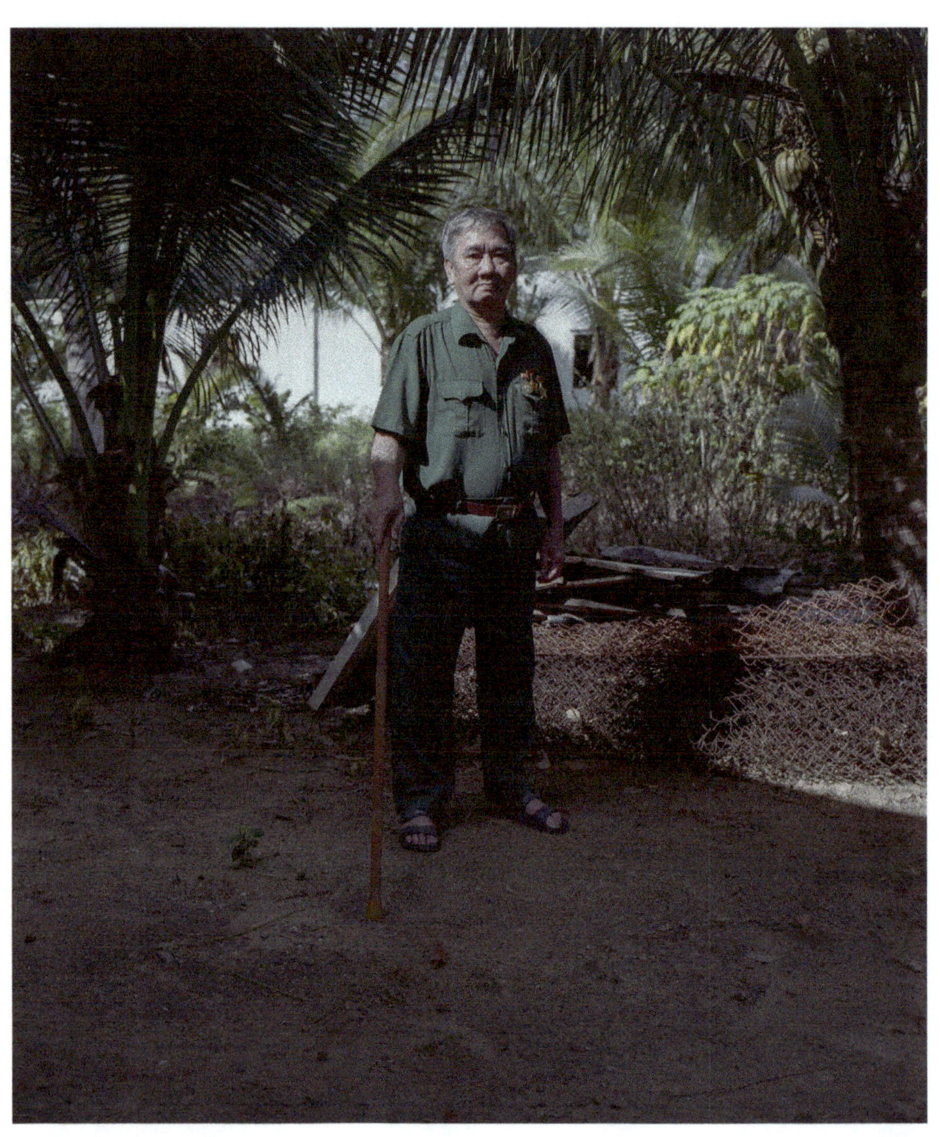

From darkness to light

From Darkness to Light: Portrait Pictures in the Bảo Tàng Côn Đảo Museum

The lighting in Bảo Tàng Côn Đảo Museum in Côn Sơn Town seems to get brighter as you walk through the rooms associated with the island's prison history. It is as if one moves from the darkest of pasts to a brighter future. Perhaps it is this which gives the narrative presented there a sense of reclamation. Throughout the different rooms displays featuring rows of portrait pictures are not uncommon, and these appear to become brighter too, partly through the inclusion of more colour photography, but also due to elevated present. Only a few are obviously prison 'mugshots', although many others may be. That of Tôn Đức Thắng, the first president of a reunified Vietnam, stands out particularly as such, showing the classic front and side profile with a name and number beneath. Others are clearly not and depict smiling faces in natural poses, such as the charming image of Cao Nguyên Loi, positioned below the maps that he drew to assist the Congressional visit to locate the Tiger Cages at Côn Sơn prison in 1970. Despite this variance there is a definite shift in the presentation of the various portrait pictures as one moves through the museum which complements the narrative of reclamation. Early on portraits are presented in partially illuminated glass cases on stark black walls. Almost all are men dressed in suits, traditional dress or military attire, and most expressions are stern and impassive. These do not bear the classic hollow, haunted look commonly associated with prison mugshots. Yet there is a seriousness which combines with the black surround and the smartness of dress to create an impression of stoic determination in the face of darkness and oppression. There is pride here but it is somber and it has suffered.

Further on the background shifts to shades of pastel and the interspersing of some colour photographs softens the still often expressionless images. More smiles can be seen, though, and more softer, female faces. In one display portrait pictures appear alongside extracts of handwriting, an individual trait which, like the face, has the capacity to personalize and, on first glance does so, as much, if not more, than the portraits. A closer inspection shows the texts here are signed declarations against the separatist movement and so the personal of the handwriting is positioned collectively, uniting those faces shown within a particular political perspective.

Elsewhere, however, the writing of prisoners is recreated in more intimate displays of letters and poetry, as well as political expression. There are no portraits here but the writings, although silent, give a voice to former inmates that portraits cannot convey. As a non-Vietnamese speaker I cannot understand the words but their presence through the small, scrawls and loops, known to have been penned by inmates during their incarceration, allows the experience of imprisonment to resonate. And here it is the absence of portraits which contributes to a sense of collectivity. These are individuals, evident in their different slants and styles of writing, but they are united in a shared ordeal and in their need to communicate beliefs and experiences to others. The information boards strengthen this, detailing codes that were used to subvert attempts to prevent communication.

Perhaps the most striking example of resistance, though, comes from another series of portrait pictures. These are unequivocally prison 'mugshots', taken not to mark the arrest or entry of female prisoners, but as an attempt to position them as 'common' criminals, thus removing a treasured identity as political beings. The photographs followed a violent attack involving beatings and tear gas to compel the women to comply with the photography process. The shots are close up and the evidence of violent treatment is plain. Rather than succumbing to the gaze of the prison, however, the women seem to have engaged in an act of collective resistance by closing their eyes; one of the few acts of subversion remaining to them. Their captors' attempts to fix them with a particular identity at least temporarily suspended. There are hints in their expressions that tell of resistance too. A look of serenity, almost superiority, on the face of one woman, despite the presence of swelling and bruising around her eyes. In another there is anger and determination. The woman's mistreatment is marked by a missing tooth but her furrowed brows convey the effort she is making to keep her eyes closed. Each picture is deeply personal but their presentation together in rows belies the collective nature of their experiences.

It is in the final room of materials on prison history that the story of reclamation reaches its apex, before the museum moves on to consider Côn Đảo today. The walls here are a brighter peachy pastel, creating a sense of greater light. Portrait pictures are numerous and their presentation has a ceremonial and celebratory form. Whilst some images are still black and white, indeed some are missing - replaced instead with the red and gold national flag - many are colour, and smiles are more abundant. Faces are evident in the form of busts as well as photographs, and many images are presented above framed certificates embossed with a red seal. Again I cannot understand the words but the meaning does not require this. These people are marked with significance, their importance officially recognized and endorsed. The suits and military attire have shifted from stoic determination in the face of darkness to a bold presentation firmly in the light. But this is not an individual reclamation. Those depicted in the early rooms have not themselves been reclaimed. They were the nadir of this narrative, living in dark times which are not to be forgotten. What has been reclaimed is in part the nation, a strong feature of all representations within the museum, particularly through the text; unsurprising at a site so central to the struggle for national independence.

What the portraits add to this narrative is the sense that the people as a whole - collectively - have been reclaimed. Their presence personalizes, but not in an individualistic way, instead acting as a reminder that the people are the nation. There are voices which are missing, of course, and the consensus on which this narrative of collective reclamation relies is undoubtedly more fractured in reality. But the portraits add an important humanizing element to a very political story in which combined effort was undoubtedly pivotal.

-Maryse Tennant

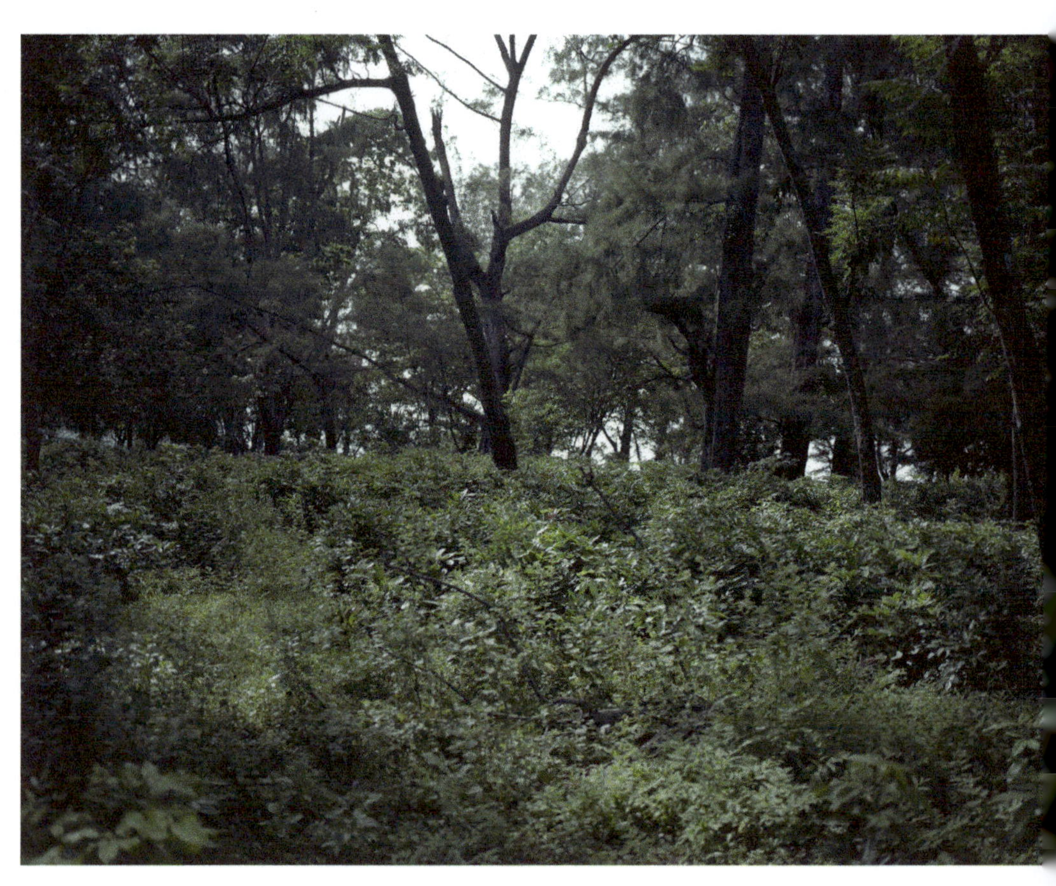

Nature reserve

Nature reserve

Former prison islands present a complex set of heritage. As Keitumetse, McAtackney and Sentata (2011) have argued they include the physical structures of the ruins, the intangibility of the human experience and stories and they are often sites of rich and diverse natural heritage. Their natural ecologies can be as rich and unique as their human heritage and many former prison islands are also protected nature conservation areas. Two of the more prominent examples are Robben Island in South Africa which has been declared a nature conservation area and Coiba Prison Island in Panama, which was turned into Coiba National Park and listed as a UNESCO World Heritage Site in 2005, after the last convict was released.

Like many other prison islands Côn Đảo archipelago is biologically-diverse. Its tropical forest contains a number of species of flora and fauna unique to the archipelago and its coastal zone is home to abundant variety of marine animals, including turtles and dugongs, and several species of clams. To protect this unique natural heritage the Côn Đảo National Park was established in 1993, 18 years after the prison closed in 1975. The national park comprises a land area of approximately 60 square kilometres. It includes large areas of Côn Sơn, the largest and only inhabited island of 16 islands and all the uninhabited islands, together with a coastal marine zone of around 140 square kilometres (CDNP, nd: online

In the poem *Breaking rocks on Con Dao* (cited earlier), the entire island is described as a prison. However, like many former prison islands (Keitumetse, McAtackney and Sentata 2011), natural and cultural environment on Côn Đảo are interpreted separately. One example of this is the So Ray plantation, which is part of Côn Đảo Natural Park. During French colonial times the plantation used to be a site of forced labour, were prisoners had to build an orchard and plant crops to produce food for the French rulers. Today one can find 20 hectares of endemic and rare trees that create a habitat and a source of natural food for wild animals such as black squirrels, long-tailed monkeys and lizards. Plans of reforestation of the plantation were put into practice when one third of the forest area was destroyed during storm Linda in 1997. However, the colonial history of the plantation is barely discussed. Following the path that leads to the plantation one can find interpretation panels on the natural heritage of the island, specifically an introduction to the tropical rainforest and the different kind of trees that can be found in the forest, such as the Banyan tree. Once one reaches the top and the plantation ruins, an interpretation panel briefly informs the visitor about the former plantation and the reforestation project.

How does this separation of nature and culture influence how visitor experience Côn Đảo Natural Park and the prison landscape? Could an in-depth reflection on the colonial history and how colonialism played a part in changing the environment on the island contribute to a better understanding of the unique natural heritage of prison islands? Would an integrated interpretation add to a comprehension of prisoners' experiences?

Katharina Massing

References

Keitumetse, Susan, McAtackney, Laura and Sentata, Gobopaone, 'Memory and Identity as Elements of Heritage Tourism in Southern Africa', in *Cultures and Globalization: Heritage, Memory and Identity*, edited by Helmut K Anheier and Yudhishthir Raj Isar (London, Sage Publications, 2011, pp157-168)

CDNP, 2018, CDNP (nd) 'About Con Dao National Park', online at: http://www.condaopark.com.vn/en/about-con-dao-national-park.html (accessed October 27th 2018).

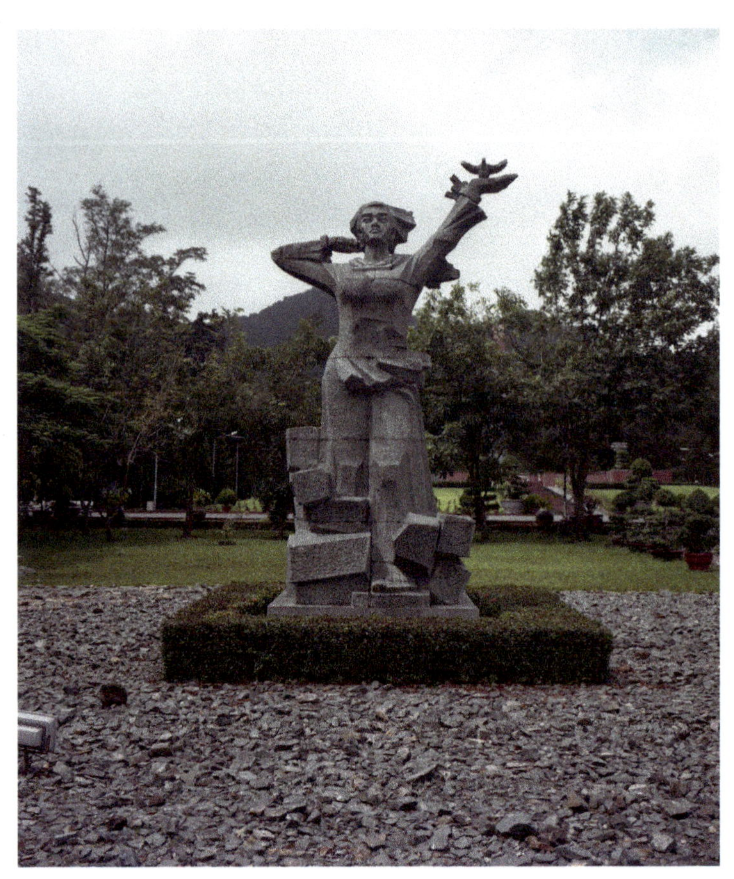

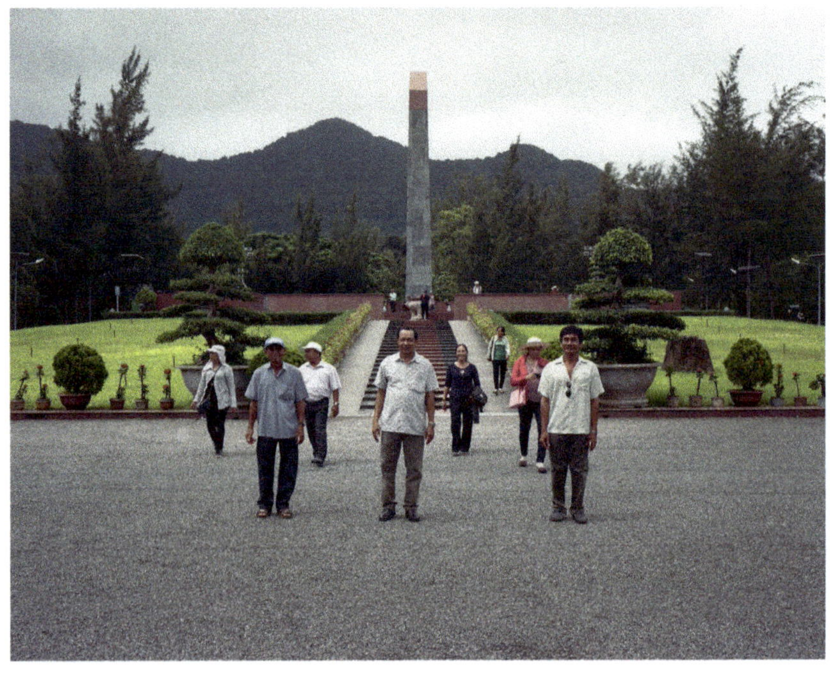

The carceral archipelago of the dead

The carceral archipelago of the dead: on the singularity of Hàng Dương cemetery

In his book *L'Archipel des morts* (1989), the anthropologist Jean-Didier Urbain describes how visiting the cemetery remains one of the most effective means of understanding another culture. Cemeteries are sites in which we can explore the dynamics of remembering and forgetting, the relationship between the living and the dead, and the ways in which engrained social values can persist beyond the grave. Studies of dark tourism have regularly explored the role of these places of burial in the range of leisure practices focused on death and suffering, in particular those relating to the First World War in north France or at Gallipoli in Turkey (Winter, 2011). Although several have attempted to separate cemeteries from dark tourism, claiming that visiting them belongs to 'similar practices as pilgrimage' (Lennon and Foley, 2000: 14-16), graveyards in city locations such as New Orleans have nevertheless played an increasingly important role in studies of the phenomenon (Stanonis, 2012). There exists an Association of Significant Cemeteries in Europe (http://www.significantcemeteries.org/), the role of which is to promote the heritage dimensions of these sites. In his catalogue of 'death and macabre related tourist sites', Philip Stone includes 'dark resting places' (Stone, 2006: 154-55; see also, Young and Light, 2016). He uses this term to designate cemeteries characterized by the Romantic and Gothic aesthetic with which they are often associated and restored as visitor attractions in a context of urban regeneration. Rachael Raine has developed this approach by identifying the multiple motivations of those who visit burial grounds, ranging from devotion and curiosity to a quest for historical knowledge and more straightforward sightseeing (Raine, 2013).

There has been less attention to cemeteries, however, in the specific context of prison tourism. Although many reflections on penal heritage focus specifically - and understandably - on prisons and other sites of captivity, Urbain's thesis regarding sites of burial considered in their own right is equally pertinent for engagement with cultures of incarceration. Few have addressed the ways in which the presence and absence of cemeteries within or in the vicinity of historic penal sites now form a significant part of heritage practices. Despite the archaeological interest in prison cemeteries evident, for example, at Spike Island near Cork, this is absent from the literature on visitor practices to these sites. The otherwise comprehensive 1,051 pages of *The Palgrave Handbook of Prison Tourism* (2017) does not, for example, contain an essay on burial locations in prisons.

The prison cemetery provides, however, an eloquent insight into the hierarchies of prison life, the dehumanizing conditions behind prison walls, and the memorial meanings and accompanying afterlives of penal sites. As the prison stock of the UK is sold off and often passes into private hands, the unmarked graves of the once incarcerated provide a physical reminder of the histories of these places. The adaptive reuse of these sites as flats, hotels and museums is still often delayed as developers discover human remains and are obliged to negotiate the ethical and archaeological challenges these pose.

In my own travels around prisons and penal colonies, I am regularly drawn to the places within these sites where the dead have been buried and their restriction to a physical context of incarceration perpetuated beyond the grave. They are equally a source of attraction for those seekers of the paranormal who frequent disused prisons, but what interests me instead is their specific memorial function, the relative preservation or ruination to which they are subjected, and what these processes tell us about the meanings and roles of penal heritage sites in the present. At times, these places are clearly signalled and carefully protected: the French Prisoner of War Cemetery at HMP Dartmouth, constructed in the 1860s to commemorate the French Prisoners of War who died during the Napoleonic Wars, is now designated as a site of special historic interest; the Isle of the Dead at Port Arthur in Tasmania is a key part of the tour of this UNESCO world heritage site, a telling illustration of the social segregation that persisted beyond the grave (convicts were buried here in mostly unmarked graves at the island's southern end; the elevated northern part was reserved for free and military burials, marked by headstones); and cemeteries remain prominent at Angola prison, the Louisiana State Penitentiary, where the majority of inmates still die while incarcerated and where ornate rituals accompany their funerals. On occasion, however, identifying these sites requires some imagination, especially when they relate less to formal cemeteries than to informal burial grounds. The final resting place of Haitian revolutionary leader Toussaint Louverture at the Château de Joux in the French Jura was a common grave, disturbed as the castle was extended in the century after his death, meaning that only a symbolic crate of earth could be returned in his memory to the national pantheon in Port-au-Prince. Elsewhere, the sites of cemeteries may still be identified, but traces of the dead have long disappeared. The remains of most convicts who died in the French penal colony of New Caledonia were buried in unmarked graves: the location of the cemetery on the hill above the penitentiary at Nouville (formerly the Ile de Nou) has been forgotten; the *cimetière des bagnards* in the forest at Prony on the south of the island is identified but any evidence of the prisoners' graves has been erased by the passage of time; and at the same location, the *cimetière des gardiens* is distinguished only by the crumbling seashells that once served as tombstones. Such neglect stands in stark contrast to other cemeteries in the islands that serve as *lieux de mémoire*: in the midst of the postcolonial penal ruination on the *Ile des pins* is the well-tended *cimetière des déportés*, where a number of Communards are interred; and just south of Bourail on Grande Terre is the Arab cemetery of Nessadiou, a key focus for the contemporary New Caledonian community of North African heritage, a number of whose ancestors - deported for their involvement in the El Mokrani revolt in Kabylie in 1871 - are buried here.

We are invited increasingly to think about the global histories of transportation and incarceration - and the interconnected traces of these histories that remain (see Anderson, 2018). As you will have understood, I am struck by the role that cemeteries play in this emerging carceral archipelago. In such a context, Hàng Dương Cemetery on Côn Sơn island is unique, in part because the practices of burial in penal colonies were evidently different from those in domestic prisons, but also because of the palimpsestic nature of this place and the symbolic role it has acquired in narratives of Vietnamese national memory. In terms of the other sites I have discussed, Hàng Dương is one of those that has been restored and is now carefully curated; it attracts visitors with a range of motivations; but its memorial function and entanglement with the *bagne* it served is very different. Situated a short walk out of town, its relationship to the seven main sites of the prison is a symbiotic one. The histories of torture, deprivation and dehumanization central to the narratives of incarceration elsewhere on the island are transcended - and find their ultimate justification - here.

Hàng Dương is not the only site of this sort relating to the prisons on Côn Sơn. Opposite the Separated Cow Shed on Võ Thị Sáu Street is the island's first burial ground (known as Bãi Sọ Người) in which around 100 prisoners killed following an insurrection in July 1862 (a month after the deportation here of the first inmates by the French) were buried alongside the twenty survivors who had been forced to dig their graves; The Hàng Keo was the original burial ground in the French *bagne*, now transformed into a space of remembrance. In both cases, human remains discovered have been reinterred at Hàng Dương (Hayward and Tran, 2014: 118). The site at Bãi Sọ Người - marked now by a more recent memorial - is a reminder that resistance emerged as soon as imprisonment on the island began, but Hàng Dương itself is a monument to the ways in which that history of struggle against French and then U.S. imperialism lasted for over a century until the end of the Vietnam War - and beyond. Covering around 20 hectares and containing the graves of approximately 20,000 prisoners (of whom only 712 have been identified) (Hayward and Tran: 118), the site avoids the immaculate, regimented appearance of those cemeteries maintained by, for instance, the Commonwealth War Graves Commission: it is tidy, but not overly so, and the tombs - placed along several meandering paths, and radiating out from a central obelisk - coexist with nature. Many visitors come at night, when the site is highly atmospheric, not for the sensationalist reasons that motivate many nocturnal prison tours, but because this is considered an auspicious time to hold vigils for the dead. The cemetery becomes then a space of socialization as well as of paying homage; those visiting burn incense, offer rice wine and cigarettes to the martyrs. The graves of key historical figures such as Lê Hồng Phong (second leader of the Communist Party of Vietnam) and Nguyễn An Ninh (writer, activist and revolutionary) become the focus of attention, but of particular interest is the tomb of Võ Thị Sáu, the teenage guerrilla executed by the French in 1952 at the age of 19, after spending a single night incarcerated at the police station on the island. One of the few extant photographs of this national martyr - in effect, her mugshot - adorns many of the souvenirs on sale on Côn Sơn. Võ Thị Sáu's tomb is now an elaborate marble construction, but built into it are the more roughly hewn grave stones that originally indicated this site, a subtle reminder of the solidarity between the incarcerated who even in the midst of conflict, when such markers were discouraged, already sought to transform a site of suffering into one of commemoration. In the context of this cemetery, Võ Thị Sáu has been elevated to the status of 'secular revolutionary "saint"' (Hayward and Tran: 118). Those coming to pray now bring offerings: fruit, flowers, incense, even whole roasted pigs.

Hàng Dương encapsulates the specificity of tourism to Côn Sơn: unlike at many other heritage sites in Vietnam, domestic visitors outnumber international tourists by a significant proportion; at the same time, the dark tourism with which much penal heritage is associated coexists here alongside memorial tourism, with the former in fact largely eclipsed by the latter. In the carceral archipelago, Côn Sơn is distinct from most other penal colonies in that its purpose was primarily if not exclusively political. As such, Hàng Dương - arguably now constructed as the prison-island's focal point - is very different from many of those penal 'dark heritage' sites discussed above, where the remains of the incarcerated are subject to systematic neglect or relegated to the past. The cemetery is a shrine: to the prisoners who died, to the martyrs they became in dying, to resistance, to the struggle against imperialism. It embodies a clear teleology, leading from the suffering in the tiger cages to ultimate liberation and independence. The site includes a souvenir shop and café, meaning that the infrastructure of (thana)tourism is prominent, but Hàng Dương is far removed from the 'dark resting places' that Stone and others describe. It is focused more on what Hayward and Tran call 'commemorational tourism' (116). The presence of foreigners is tolerated here, met more with indifference than any hostility. Actively harnessed to national ideology, this meticulously orchestrated *lieu de mémoire* represents uses of the past that often seem absent elsewhere in Vietnam; but part of Hàng Dương's attraction remains the elevation of highly personal stories through which collective sentiment is channelled. On Võ Thị Sáu's grave is a stylized white marble medallion depicting her face; the lips on this portrait are invariably decorated with lipstick, an unexpectedly and subversively feminine touch that underlines the extent to which Hàng Dương continues to speak directly to its primarily Vietnamese visitors, whether veterans or those of a generation born long after the war.

Charles Forsdick

References

Anderson, Clare, (ed.), *A Global History of Convicts and Penal Colonies* (London: Bloomsbury Academic, 2018).

Lennon, John and Foley, Malcolm, *Dark Tourism: The Attraction of Death and Disaster* (London: Continuum, 2000).

Raine, Rachael, 'A dark tourist spectrum', *International Journal of Culture, Tourism and Hospitality Research*, 7.3 (2013), 242-56.

Stanonis, Anthony J., 'Dead but delightful: tourism and memory in New Orleans cemeteries', in Karen L. Cox (ed.), *Destination Dixie: Tourism and Southern History* (Gainesville, FL: University Press of Florida, 2012).

Stone, Philip R., 'A dark tourism spectrum: towards a typology of death and macabre related tourist sites, attractions and exhibitions', *Tourism*, 54.2 (2006), 145-60.

Urbain, Jean-Didier, *L'Archipel des morts: le sentiment de la mort et les dérives de la mémoire dans les cimetières d'Occident* (Paris: Plon, 1989).

Wilson, Jaqueline Z., Hodgkinson, Sarah, Piche, Justin and Walby, Kevin (eds), *The Palgrave Handbook of Prison Tourism* (New York, NY: Palgrave, 2017).

Winter, Caroline, 'First World War cemeteries: insights from visitor books', *Tourism Geographies*, 13.3 (2011), 462-79.

Young, Craig and Light, Duncan, 'Interrogating spaces of and for the dead as "alternative space": cemeteries, corpses and sites of Dark Tourism,' *International Journal of Social Research*, 6.2 (2016), 61-72.

Acknowledgments

The photographer, Charles Fox, would like to thank the former prisoners of Con Dao who so kindly shared their experiences and time, Nguyễn Văn Ước, Nguyễn Văn Bảnh, Phan Hoàng Oanh, Nguyễn Xuân Viên and Nguyễn Thị Ni. I would also like to thank Lê Thị Thảo Quyên from "Hội người tù kháng chiến huyện Côn Đảo" (The Association of former political prisoners in Con Dao) for all her and assistance.

The exhibition team would like to thank colleagues at NTU including Mohamed Gamal Abdelmonem, Andy Gritt, Angela Brown, Tom Fisher, Neville Stankley, Duncan Grewcock, Ross Smith. Thanks also go to the team at the National Justice Museum including Bev Baker and Lauren Sulley. Special thanks go to colleagues at Ton Duc Thang University especially Dr Kim Phung Dang, John Hutnyk, Bùi Loan Thùy, Dr Lê Thị Mai, Nguyễn Phú Quốc Nam. Additional thanks go to Tim Lustig, Suzanne McGowan, Steve Legg, students on the MA in Museum and Heritage Development, the hotel staff at Nha Khach Con Dao, Dang Uyen Vo at the Ton Duc Thang Museum in Ho Chi Minh City and Gilles Poizat at the Archives Nationales d'Outre Mer.

Generous financial support was provided by NTU School of Arts and Humanities, School of Art and Design and the Global Heritage Research Theme. Funding for the workshop 'A Poetics of Space: Ecology and Heritage in Vietnam' was provided by the British Academy as part of a Newton mobility exchange between Nottingham Trent University and Ton Duc Thang University in Ho Chi Minh City.

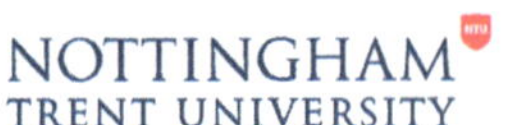

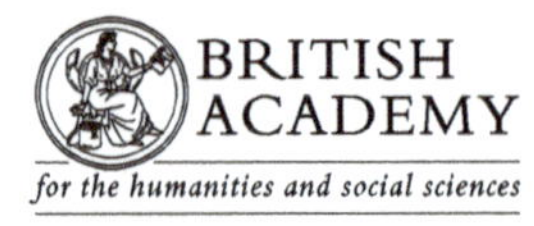

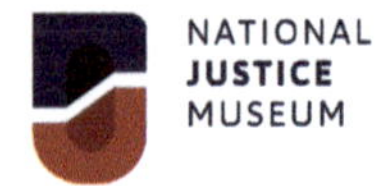

www.ingramcontent.com/pod-product-compliance
Lightning Source LLC
LaVergne TN
LVHW052357100826
845147LV00013B/862
* 9 7 8 0 9 5 7 1 4 7 0 2 7 *